ANIMAL BATHS

Wild & Wonderful Ways
Animals Get Clean!

ANIMAL BATHS

Wild & Wonderful Ways Animals Get Clean!

BY BETH FIELDING

ILLUSTRATIONS BY SUSAN GREENELSH

EarlyLight Books
Waynesville, North Carolina, USA

Cataloging Information

Fielding, Beth.
    Animal baths: Wild and wonderful ways animals get clean!/ written by Beth
        Fielding; illustrated by Susan Greenelsh.
        48 p. : col. ill. ; 20 cm.
    Summary: Explores the range of behavior used by animals from a range of taxa,
        including mammals, insects, reptiles, birds, and fish. Also includes
        morphology information.
    LC: QL 751
    Dewey: 591.5
    ISBN-13: 978-0-9797455-2-2   (alk. paper)
    ISBN-10: 0-9797455-2-7 (alk. paper)
        Animal behavior—Juvenile literature
        Baths – Juvenile literature
        Animals – Habits and behavior

Art Director: Cindy LaBrecht
Project Editor: Dawn Cusick
Copy Editor: Susan Brill

10 9 8 7 6 5 4 3 2 1

First edition

Published by EarlyLight Books, Inc.
1436 Dellwood Road
Waynesville, NC 28786

Distributed by BookMasters Inc.

ISBN-13: 978-0-9797455-2-2
ISBN-10: 0-9797455-2-7

CONTENTS

MUD, DUST, & POOP (YES, POOP!)   6
Some animals get really dirty to get clean!

TONGUES, CLAWS, & TEETH   18
Who needs a washcloth and soap?

SCAMMING, SHEDDING, & SLAMMING!   30
Get someone else to clean you, or just ditch your dirty skin!

SOME ANIMALS GET REALLY DIRTY TO GET CLEAN!

YOU PROBABLY only take one bath a day. And if you don't take a bath today, you might be a little stinky tomorrow, but you'll be okay. For wild animals, though, taking baths helps keep them healthy.

Dirty skin, feathers, and fur are good homes for parasites and bacteria that can make animals sick. Parasites and bacteria can live on our skin and make us sick, too, but we can go to a doctor for medicine and animals can not.

In this chapter, you will meet animals that use mud, dirt, dust, water—and even poop—to get clean. The next time you're in a shower or bathtub using a bar of soap or shampoo, imagine what it would be like to roll in mud or dust instead!

MUD, DUST, & POOP

(YES, POOP!)

ELEPHANT BATHS

ELEPHANTS TAKE take three types of baths. When they're near water, they use their trunks like a giant hose and spray water all over themselves.

Elephants also use their trunks to take dust baths. They suck the dust into their trunks and then blow it over their bodies. The dust helps keep bugs off their skin.

When they want to cool off on a hot day, elephants take mud baths. The cool mud keeps the sun off and makes them feel better. When the mud dries and falls off, it takes old skin and bugs with it.

RHINOCEROS BATHS

RHINOS LOVE mud baths. The thick mud protects their skin from the sun and heat, just like it does for elephants. When the mud dries and cracks, biting insects fall off their skin.

If the idea of a mud bath makes you crinkle your nose and say, "ewwwwww," look at it from a rhino's point of view. They have ticks on their backs that are bigger than the purple grapes your mom buys at the grocery store. You would take a mud bath, too, to get rid of ticks that big!!!

Rhinos have several other ways to get insects off their skin. They take dust baths or rub their skin against trees.

 Rhinos also have hungry friends—egret and oxpecker birds— that ride on their backs and pull bugs from their skin.

ZEBRA BATHS

JUST LIKE elephants and rhinos, zebras like to take dust and mud baths. After they roll in the dust, zebras shake their bodies back and forth like a dog does after a bath. When the dust falls out, so do small parasites and dirt. When the mud dries and cracks in the sun, the zebra's shedding fur falls out with the mud, too.

Zebras also clean each other by using their large teeth to scrape the fur around the shoulders, necks, and backs of other zebras. Sometimes two zebras will clean each other at the same time. Usually, zebras will only clean a family member or a member of their herd—they don't usually clean a stranger.

Have you ever seen a horse roll in the dust? Horses are close relatives of zebras, and often clean themselves the same way zebras do even though they have owners who spend a lot of time grooming them.

BIRD BATHS

MANY BIRDS take sun baths. They find a safe place (without predators!) to stretch their wings out flat so the sun's rays can reach their feathers. Heat energy from the sun works like a disinfectant soap to kill bacteria and parasites in the birds' feathers.

Some birds also take dust or sand baths. Just like many furry mammals, the birds roll through the dust or sand so it gets deep into their feathers. Next, they shake their feathers so that dead skin and small bugs fall out with the dirt. To finish a bath, birds carefully "preen" each feather. Some scientists think the sand and dust helps absorb extra preening oil from the birds' feathers.

Birds also like to clean themselves in water, and people like to watch them splash their feathers in a bird bath.

TURKEY VULTURE BATHS

SUPPOSE YOU are a turkey vulture and your favorite dinner is the dead body of a once-sick or rotting animal? And suppose that rotten flesh—and all the germs in it—gets all over your legs and on the top of your head every time you eat? How would you clean up after dinner?

Turkey vultures clean their legs by squirting poop all over them! The poop contains special antibacterial chemicals that work the same way bathroom soap works to kill germs. Heat energy from the sun kills bacteria and germs on top of the turkey vulture's head.

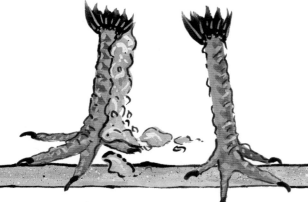

WHO NEEDS A WASHCLOTH & SOAP?

ANIMALS DON'T have towels and washcloths like people do to help clean themselves. Instead, some animals use parts of their bodies—tongues, claws, teeth, or beaks—to clean their fur and feathers.

Birds and mammals can take 40 or 50 baths a day! Birds take so many baths because if their feathers are dirty, they may not be able to fly fast enough to avoid a predator or catch enough insects for dinner. And it's not just the grown-up animals that take a lot of baths. Some baby bats spend almost all day cleaning their fur.

So the next time you climb into a shower or bath, be glad you can use a washcloth—instead of your tongue, claws, teeth, or beak—to clean your skin. And be extra glad you only have to take one bath a day!

TONGUES,
CLAWS,
& TEETH

CAT BATHS

CATS BATHE themselves by licking their fur. A cat's tongue has lots of small bumps on it (called papillae), and each bump has a small hook at the end. The papillae hooks act like combs when a cat licks itself, removing loose fur, dirt, and food particles from the cat's fur. Cats also lick their paws and use the wet paws like a washcloth to clean their faces and heads.

Tongue baths do more for cats than keep them clean. When it's hot outside, tongue baths help cats cool off. When it's cold, tongue baths smoothe the fur hairs close together to keep in body heat.

Baths also help cats in another special way. Cat

saliva has scent molecules that leave a unique smell on the cat's fur. This smell helps mom cats recognize their kittens and helps lions recognize each other in the wild.

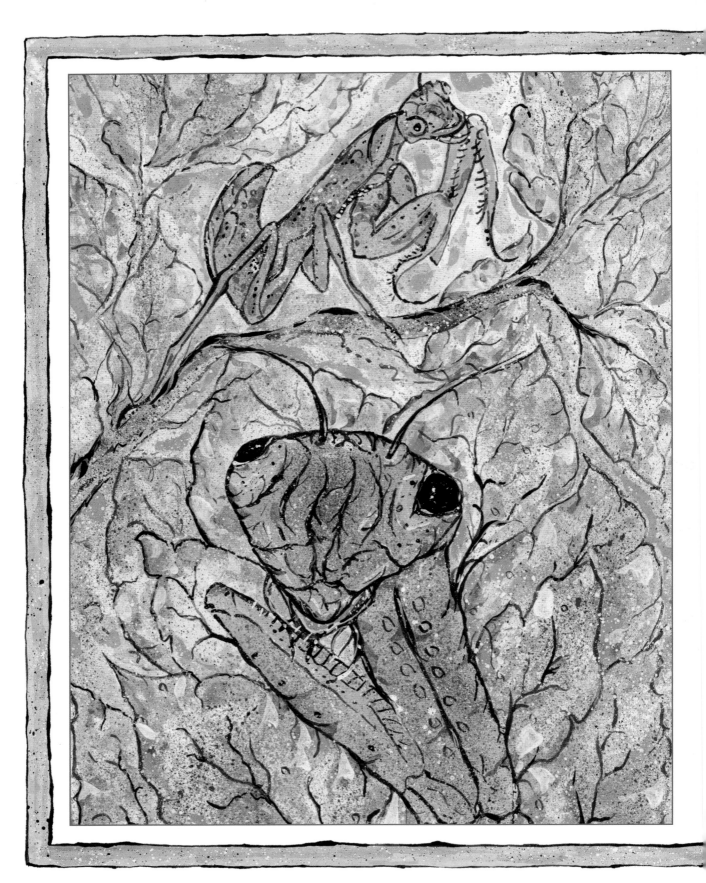

PRAYING MANTIS BATHS

PRAYING MANTISES have lots of body parts that need special cleaning. Their ears are on their antennae—really!—so it's important to keep them very clean. To clean their thread-like antennae, they bend them down from the tops of their heads and run them over their tongues.

Mantises also use their tongues and mouthparts to clean between the sharp ridges on their front legs. Mantises use the ridges on their legs to tightly hold bugs such as flies and katydids while they eat them, which can make their legs slimy and sticky.

Some people think praying mantises look like house cats when they're cleaning themselves!

SQUIRREL BATHS

SQUIRRELS SPEND most of their time doing two things: eating and bathing. To take a sun bath, squirrels spread their bodies out flat on the ground so the sun's cleaning heat can shine on their heads, backs, and legs. Squirrels also take dust baths and sand baths by rolling in the sand to rub it into their fur and then shaking it off.

Squirrels also clean their fur by licking their front paws with their tongues and then using their wet paws like a washcloth to clean their faces and necks.

Most squirrels have very bushy tails and work hard to keep them clean. To clean their tails, squirrels bring their tails up to their mouths and use their teeth like a hairbrush to clean their tail fur.

BAT BATHS

BATS USE their tongues to clean their faces, their feet, and their ears—just like cats and squirrels. To clean their wings, bats use the hooked area in their thumbs like a comb to smooth their fur and remove small bugs and parasites.

Most bats clean themselves for hours every day. Some types of bats, such as female vampire bats, also clean (or groom) other female bats. When one female finishes grooming another, the bat who was groomed says "thank-you" by puking up some of her dinner and giving it to the groomer.

The next time your mom helps you clean your hair or your skin, be glad you don't have to say thank-you with a little puke!

PORCUPINE BATHS

PORCUPINES HAVE have a unique cleaning problem. Their backs and tails are covered with sharp spines, known as quills, that are used to protect them against predators. An average porcupine may have as many as 30,000 quills that need cleaning!

Since it would take a long, long time to clean 30,000 quills, and since it would really, really, really hurt if sharp spines poked their tongues, porcupines have a special trick to keep clean. First, they squeeze the muscles around the quills to stand them up straight. Then they shake their bodies so the dirt falls off and loose spines fall out!

Porcupines wash the areas that don't have any spines on them—their faces, paws, and tummies—with their tongues and their paws. They also use their big teeth and their claws to groom their thick fur.

GET SOMEONE ELSE TO CLEAN YOU, OR JUST DITCH YOUR DIRTY SKIN!

SOME ANIMALS use other animals to help them get clean. Crocodiles and giraffes, for example, let birds eat bugs in their teeth and fur. It's a good deal for both animals: the crocodiles and giraffes get cleaned and the birds get food!

Turtles and big fish get cleaned in a similar way—smaller fish eat algae and parasites from their scales and shells. Some birds also get cleaned this way, letting ants and other bugs move through their feathers to eat small parasites.

Snakes, frogs, and lizards clean themselves by taking sun baths or by shedding their old, dirty skin. And some fish have a really cool way of cleaning their scales: they slam themselves against rocks to make dirt and parasites fall off!

So the next time you can't reach a dirty spot on your back or have something stuck between your teeth, try getting a bird or a fish to give you a bath!

SCAMMING, SHEDDING, & SLAMMING

BUFFALO & ANTELOPE BATHS

SUPPOSE YOU were a buffalo or an antelope and had lots of bugs and parasites biting and sucking blood on your back. You don't have hands to scratch or pull the bugs off, and you don't have a mom or dad to help scrub you clean. What would you do?

Oxpecker birds use their beaks to clean bugs and other parasites from large animals. After they pull the bugs out of the animal's fur, the oxpeckers eat the bugs for food. The birds get so much food from buffalos and antelopes that they often spend all day standing on the big animals' heads, backs, and necks. Sometimes buffalos and antelopes walk around with a small flock of birds on top of them!

Oxpecker birds eat bugs and parasites from rhinos and giraffes, too.

ANTING BIRD BATHS

MORE THAN 250 different types of birds use ants instead of soap to clean their feathers. To take an ant bath, the bird either kicks an ant mound or lies down on top of it. The ants climb onto the bird and spray their defense chemical (formic acid) into the bird's feathers. Scientists think the formic acid kills small bugs and bacteria living in the bird's feathers.

Some birds take another type of ant bath. Instead of waiting for the ants to come to them, they reach down and pick up some ants with their beaks, then rub the ants on their feathers. Some birds rub millipedes, wasps, and bees into their feathers instead of ants. These types of baths are called "anting."

CHIMPANZEE BATHS

INSTEAD OF TAKING baths or showers, chimpanzees and baboons groom each other's fur with their fingers.

The chimp who does the grooming may spend hours looking through another chimp's fur for bugs, leaves, and sticky things like tree sap or dried food and mud.

When the grooming chimp finds a bug, he or she looks at it very carefully. If it's a good-tasting bug, the grooming chimp eats it. If it's a bad-tasting bug, the grooming chimp kills the bug by squishing it against a leaf.

Sometimes the chimp who does the grooming is the mom or a friend. And sometimes the groomer is someone who wants a favor, a special treat, or who just wants everyone who lives with him to be happy.

SNAKE, FROG, & LIZARD BATHS

IF YOU WERE a snake, you would never have to take a bath again! When snake skin gets old and dirty, snakes rub their faces against something hard, like a rock, until the skin tears. Then they just crawl out of their old skin!

Some frogs shed their skin the same way you take off a shirt. They start at the bottom of their bodies and move the dead skin up and over their heads. When they're done shedding their skin, they eat it! Imagine if your mom gave you dead frog skin for an afternoon snack—yum yum! Actually, frogs don't eat their skin because it tastes good. They eat the skin so their bodies can recycle the water and nutrients that are in it.

Most lizards shed their skin in small pieces, and some lizards eat their old skin the same way frogs eat their skin.

TURTLE BATHS

A CLEAN SHELL is very important for a turtle to stay healthy. Turtles that live in freshwater streams and ponds sit in the sun for hours every day to keep warm and clean their shells.

Most ocean turtles don't have places to sun themselves, so they use another way to keep their shells clean. They swim near coral reefs and look for fish such as angelfish and damselfish that like to eat algae. A single turtle may have lots of fish eating algae from its shell at the same time. If the turtle swims around, the fish will follow!

Areas on coral reefs that have lots of algae-eating fish are called "cleaning stations."

FISH BATHS

TURTLES ARE NOT the only animals that go to underwater cleaning stations. Large fish let small coral reef fish, called cleaner wrasse, remove parasites, dead scales, and mucus from their bodies. The coral trout even allows the cleaner wrasse to go inside its mouth and clean its teeth!

Cleaner wrasse do a special dance, bobbing their heads up and down and moving their bodies. When the big fish see the dance, they come over for a cleaning instead of eating the smaller fish. Scientists have done research that shows the fish that visit cleaning stations are much healthier than fish that do not.

Another way some fish clean their scales is by body slamming rocks! Parasites and dead scales fall off or stick to the rock.

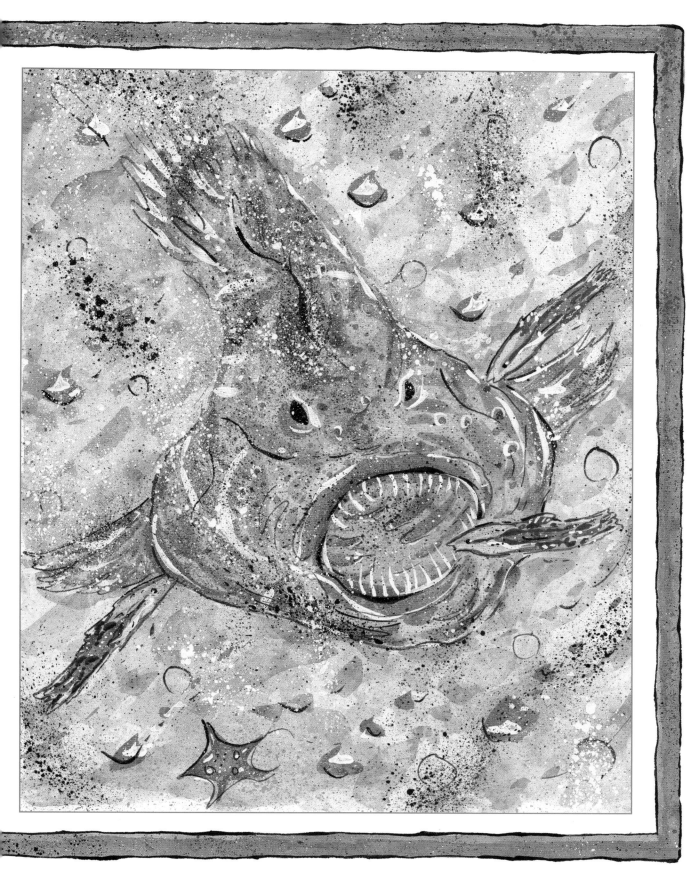

CORAL BATHS

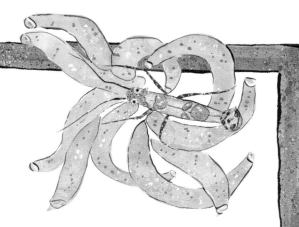

UNDERWATER CORAL reefs are created by millions of tiny animals living together. Their hard, outside surfaces, called exoskeletons, often have algae growing on them. The algae can make breathing difficult for the coral animals, and also makes it hard for young coral animals to grow. So how do coral get clean?

Colorful parrotfish clean the algae off the coral by chewing it with their strong, beak-like teeth. The parrotfish gets dinner and the coral can breathe and grow better.

Sometimes parrotfish bite off part of the coral's exoskeleton with the algae. It doesn't hurt the coral and the fish spit it out. These tiny pieces of exoskeleton create lots of soft, white sand under the coral. Scientists say that just one parrotfish can make almost a ton of sand in two months!

PEOPLE BATHS

JUST LIKE ANIMALS, people need to be clean. Some kids love to get in the bathtub or the shower. They have fun playing with bubbles and toys. Other kids cry or hide when Mom says it's bath time.

People use soap and washcloths to clean their skin, and shampoo to wash their hair. Animals can't go shopping for soap and shampoo in the grocery store. Instead, they have lots of other ways to get clean.

When you're done with your bath, you probably use a fluffy towel to dry off and then put on your pajamas. Have you ever seen a bird or an elephant use a towel or wear pajamas? Instead, animals sit in the sun or roll in the grass to dry off.

The next time Mom says it's time for a bath, think about all the ways animals get clean!

INDEX